Year
of
Healing

Year of Healing

A Collection of Poems in 2020

Kristin Roark

For My Boys:
Daniel, Aidan, Jude, Elijah

May you always know how deeply
you are loved.

Contents

Contents

"Arise, shine, for your light has come."
Isaiah 60:1

Winter

December

God spoke
in a dream
like he has
like he often
seems to do
He said
2020 will be
a year of healing for you,
the body, soul and spirit kind—
the piñata kind of healing
wrapped in scripture
bursting, bat to rib
shiny gold upon thy head,
me—
leaping,
weeping,
scooping it up,
carrying it home
and pouring over
every
Holy
word.

February

Hiding in tight spaces:
closets, bathrooms, cars—
anywhere with locks on doors.

Call it what you will:
lack of sunshine
hormones
mental illness
change.

Week three of:
body aches
fever
isolation
dread.

Year of Healing

       more like

Year of Disease.

Gray Skies

I'm slipping
under the covers
and over my head,
a noose-neck suffocation
into the deep-throated dark.

Heavy lids
shut tight to block
black-ocean waves, white
and foaming at the mouth,
tossing body back to sea.

One quick slice,
of a knife on taut rope,
skin snap into the whirlwind,
silenced now. There, there—
a thousand worlds away.

A Prayer

Where are you
when I feel nothing
and everything
all at once.

When I take the blade
across my wrist to
release and feel
fleshy tug and pull
against the skin sack
on my bones.

The flesh often wins
the battle of my mind
and so I wonder
in the wrestle
where you are
in this time.

An Offering

Here's my heart, O God
I'm ripping it out of chest
handing it over.
It's not elegant,
not on a fancy platter
with plump figs and greens.
No, it's quite a mess
butterflied and wide—
a heap of spoiled berries.
Throw it out with trash
or let ravens pick it clean,
have mercy on me.
God, I'm worn, numbing
the cutting, and distracting
it leaves me famished.
I'll never be clean
God, never measure up to
The One who heals me.
I'll never be kind,
God, never wait on my rage
long enough to ease.
Yet, you are kind, clean
drawing me near, a Father
running to lost heir.
Thank you for kindness
for rinsing and repeating
this bruised-apple heart.

A Life

Is this real life?
On repeat,
these words, these days.
Real and Life.
Words that wake me mid-dream,
in the still quiet dawn
before hungry, sleepy boys in pj's
go searching for the milk.
I find myself trapped
inside blank walls,
peeking through beige blinds,
to gather strength,
to burst outside,
barefoot onto grass,
to exhale, "I'm alive!"
I'm alive.
Empty lungs and,
all my breath,
for all the neighbors,
peeking through all their blinds,
feeling stuck in all their walls,
to hear a human voice say:
This is real.
And this is life.

It's OK
to feel it all.

In Hiding

For now, I'm withdrawing, dark places
collecting dust, a snow globe
on the edge.

And tomorrow,
someone will find me
scoop me up
and set me gently
into light
with laughter
or with shrieks—
with human touch.

And I'll say,
Aha—
You are
real
and this is
life.

We are here,
holding each other up—
carriers of the light.

Awake

Have you ever
seen such heartbreak
black and white,
streaming from screens,
sweaty palms,
heavy-lunged chests,
cavernous spaces for
dark webs to grow wild;
or have you considered
shutting it off,
tending to
your own wild heart,
peeking it open with bare hands,
surrendering to God,
waking to the sleepy bird song,
porch-sitting with coffee,
building canopies
in the sun?

Suffocation

Hanging in the air
a spider
crafting webs,
that wrap
around our necks,
silk bow on bone.
Ice-cold and whispering, *"six feet"*
in freezer sections
while we shelter in
tight circles.
Quickly,
quietly,
threading through the night,
lacing panic and illness
in our lungs,
face-masked,
we gasp
for air.

Another day,
Another dream.
Another chance to say,
"I see you" to the sneak-thief,
unseen destroyer,
swept out only
by the Light.

Repentance

If my heart were a flower,
not a fresh one
bursting with verve and vibrancy,

No.

If my heart were a flower,
dark and withered
drooping with a fleshy heaviness,

I'd let you reach in, bare hands, big grip
and pluck it out of my fallen-in chest
if that's what you wanted.

Go ahead. Pull it apart and pick it clean.
Petal, by wilted petal,
plip,
plip,
until my heart-flower
piles atop
onto earth,
into something new.

Or, reach in, like a surgeon,
scalpel and precision, carve it out,
if that's what you'd rather.

Go ahead. Slice the wild stem that seals
heart and marrow. Shoot by broken shoot.
snip,
snip,
and set it in a glass
on the lazy susan.

In other words,
prune my heart
so I can turn
and grow
and turn
and grow
again,
again.

In other words,

Do what you will
to shape
to doctor
heavy petal-flesh,
weary stick-bone
into pots of
spirit-filled *gold.*

Spring

Advent

I had a vision of Jesus today.
He visited, back deck in the middle of the afternoon.

There he was, in my mind's eye, brighter than the sun.
In his hands, two suitcases
fit with letters to every human
on the planet.

His face, like a light beam,
His voice, like a sword.
Hammer of hope,
as he spoke.

Prepare your heart, he said.
Make room.
Open windows.
Clear the clots.
Sweep the dirt out.
Welcome in the light—
The spirit of truth and grace.

His message, urgent, yet
it's not a harshness when he comes,
rather a softening of heart toward the Father's
great love.

Revival

Desert heat in the
late noon sun falls fiercely on
sun-cracked earth, slinging

shadows and dry air.
Breath is stifled like feelings
in sandpaper lungs.

Buried head in sand,
pale and chapped lips give way to
a war-cry, "Enough!"

A mighty wind whips
my gaze to drink in blue sky,
quenching thirst within.

Holy fire burns
my heart in a wasteland grave
now aflame for God.

Maybe this is how
Revival starts—earth and fire,
water for the parched.

Sunday

let it rain
let it pour
let the black clouds

break open
like mussels
on the shore

spilling
salt and pearls
wet earth

one drop
after heavy-ocean
drop

no sun to say
get up, shake loose
the curtains of your shell.

The woods

I go to the woods after breakfast.
It's quiet then,
aside from the twig snaps, and the spilled-
over laughter
from hurried boys, two steps ahead, one
behind, always
tumbling, always racing to keep up.

I notice the way the dappled sun-
lit path gives space
for tunnels of trees and bursts of blue-
eyed grass to stretch
up and out as if it were trying
to hug the sun.
"This is it," I call to the boys, mid-step.

A peek of past,
and future, all at once, like stepping
in the Throne Room
in the morning, dewy and so bright.
A world awaking,
expanding their holy tents for more.

I want to be
like the vine-covered tree in the woods,
unwavering,
surrounded, handing out fresh air, while
also thirsting
for space, for water, for sun. Never
alone in the middle of the forest
always at home.

Jude

Yesterday, it rained
and stopped
and rained
and stopped.

The sky shifted as quickly as
my second born changed his clothes.
And I wished the day
would make up its mind
so I could settle on my mood,
but Jude didn't mind,
he took my hand and pulled me out into
the sprinkle of the day.

I followed with a heavy sigh,
and was cooled by silver drops,
the water, soft and clean between my toes.
I watched as Jude sprang towards the rivers—
quiet waters near the drains.
Look! He splashed while turning back,
and I looked—
spirited one, dancing naked in the street.

And the rain continued to come and go,
and I thought today,
was a good day,
after all.

Rest

I need to lay
in the sun

just until
the heat burns
away the nausea

just until
I am still

hot and happy
like the belly
of the earth

just until
I spill—

golden light
smoldered in
a holy flame.

Joy

The sun—ripe and golden,
sweet cantaloupe of light
dips beneath the trees,
dripping ribbons of juice on leaves.

My joy—I imagine
is like this, yellow orb,
organic and so pure

Rising and burning there—
belly-deep, beyond the lung,
soul and skin; Glory.

But when the sun takes her
goodnight bow below the moon,
and the black night folds in
to swallow up my happy,

My joy—I imagine
is like this, blanket night—
distant and forgotten.

Will it shine, sweet fruit,
like sun again next season?
Or will it, stay hidden
under the thick peel of
the night.

Evening sun

creates and releases
light, like words
that give life
to tiny seeds
stuffed between
concrete cracks—
secret poems
for stick-clad kids
to trample 'neath their
summertime tip-toes
tipping home
for toast and story time
to do it again,
tomorrow.

Memorial Day

Monday. It was Memorial Day,
a day of remembrance,
but for whom?

And for what am I to recall now?
a shameful past, one more
injustice?

Spirit's crushed and crying, "I can't breathe"
knee to neck, hushed—heavy
under boot.

For although my skin is white, it's worn.
I'm woman, human too—
Here, I mourn.

What's next?

Sitting on the edge, my bed
grinding on my teeth, the floor
looks nice enough to fold into
let my body mold into
the hardwood,
as I wait for the other shoe
to drop.

Division,
everywhere.
Love your neighbor—no more,
it's only serve Thy Self.

And I watch from the floor,
hands over heart,
stretched lung,
groaning with the earth—
as it
all
falls
down
around me.

Summer

Bread

When the quarantine is over I go to the store.
I've been there many times before.
It's nothing new—not a novelty to finally enjoy,
but, like a newborn speckled fawn,
I fumble my way outside the womb—
foot tripping foot, wobbly-kneed, my hand
shielding sunlight as I try to recall
the way. Is it this way or that way?
Like I wasn't there last week.
And what is it that I need again?
Vegetables, olive oil, meat—
flour for the bread, to break.
And wine to toast, I suppose,
But with whom? Friends tucked away, are they
ready to leave their warm-bellied nest?
To get dressed, to drive cars, to hurry up?
I've forgotten how not to live
this sheltered-in way—
to sit and to feast and to remember.

And besides, it all feels like too much now:
the scheduling, the going out,
the filling up of days.

Red Balloon

the door is open
and I'm paralyzed.

I don't remember
how to do this

how to go
how to be

how to float
outside

here, inside
the loneliness

is wearing
me—a balloon

tied tight with
heavy thoughts

swirling in a
cloudy head

about to fly
about to pop

the door is open
and I'm paralyzed.

I don't remember
how to do this

and so,
I stay inside

tethered by tears,
red with fear,

pinned to cushion,
weights around my wrist.

Zoloft

Day fifteen. A dozen or so to go.
Chisel cement-heavy head from bed,
baby cries, "Oh, Mommy!"
I try to cling to dreams, like webs that hang
around my mind. But the light pulls
the natural world in front.
I stand up and everything hurts: the dreams,
the screams, my head, this day
and how can I say, today
Dear kids, your mommy isn't well again
I'm too dizzy to drive, to dress
to laugh, to cry. And the voice
that crawls out of my throat, my lips
could not be from me, it seems
like another is here—
a quieter one maybe, but mostly weary.
Tired of the brain zap, vertigo
foggy-head, shell of self.
I hug my baby close to chest, sweet breath
and pray that after ten odd years,
of swallowing these pills
I can quit them once and for all, in hopes
of healing, in hopes of one day
feeling like myself again.
Whoever that was, this is me—my voice,
my body, my mind, withdrawing
from Zoloft.

Friday

I almost cut myself today.
Picked up the razor
touched metal to skin
then lobbed the cheap thing
against the wall.

I fell into a ball
and rolled body back and forth
back and forth—
a rocking horse,
unhinged.

Until the sounds, like a carousel
crashed and quieted,
until the flashes of red
went white.

Anxiety

If anxiety were a choice,
I'd rather not accept it.
Rather, I'd reject it
to the curb I'd send it
with the recyclables, the green bin
so every Thursday the truck can cart it away
melt it down and mold it into something else,
something pretty—
a jar for peonies, perhaps
or a tote to carry the cherries
from farmers markets on Sundays.
Someday, I'll make a trade of sorts:
trash for purpose.
Nevertheless,
It's not a choice.
No plastic bottle to reuse,
but more, a distraction.
An intruder with a mailing address
that refuses to uproot.
And so—
my house is a mess

and this shape-shifter
presses up my cupboards,
spills over porcelain sinks,
crawls down walls, paper thin
my skin, sits within
bowls of batter
dishes clatter
crusts of bread
underfoot, tiny Lego blocks
and dirty socks,
eggshells everywhere,
cracking under pressure
spouse's sock feet skating passed
his eyes, just a glance
two headlights in the kitchen
and the truck outside
grinds away our grievances
to the junkyard
of our souls.

Once a week,
my boys have one job:
take out the recycling—

    Otherwise, I swear
    I'll throw it
    all away.

Bed

I wake up ready to crawl
back into my sheet cocoon,
burrow deep into my skin;
fall into anything—
other than the day.
No, not ready to emerge
anew. I'm worn and droopy—
left-alone flower in a pot of clay,
thirsty for a drop.

Wake me when the meds have done their job,
when I'm not a barren bucket of dried up blooms,
when my head's no longer crushed
by the weight of a house,
wake me when
it's time.

Cliché

2020 has me heart-broken,
longing to be outside,
still, here I am
baking bread
washing hands
training a puppy
singing Hamilton
homeschooling kids
rearranging furniture
attempting to run
      away,
anyway—
same as you?

Fall

The Heart

When it's all stripped away
to nothing, like water pulled
down the shower drain,

what's the seed left in
your heart, planted there to grow
the truth—you are loved?

Intercession

Where are
the people who
wake
sleepy-eyed
in the quiet
inky morning
to hear
inner ear
the hum-drumming
of the heart
beat

who heed
head in hands
on humble
hidden floors
to press
cheek to cheek
with the feathered
face of
God

the people who
labor
at home
day after
day
groaning
night upon
night
for the harvest
to come
on earth
as it is
as it always
should have been;

where are the people
who pray?

Masked

Half a step in store,
keys in a clean hand,
crinkled list in the other,
when lock-eyed with a stranger
reminds me of my blank and
naked face.

Shit. I grumble soft
back to the car to
retrieve the sad thing—saggy
cloth, sweat-stained hanging from the
rear view.

It's not supposed to
be this way, I put
the mask in place. No smile,
even if there was one to be seen.

My second grader
starts school tomorrow.
He'll meet his teacher, first time
behind a masquerade
and fist bumps.

In all of his joy,
he might not notice
the lack of warmth in the air
but I will. The way the light
used to bounce off faces, sending
beams of hope around
a room.

The way it felt to
breathe in fresh air and
cut grass after lunch. The simple
bliss of catching cool sips
from the water fountain between class.

I grab a cold cart
and clean the handles
nodding to the woman with
three kids, pushing past, a blur.
Remind me why we're doing this
again?

And we'll all keep on going,
and we'll all keep on growing,
further and further
apart.

Theatre

I was a theatre major in college—
darker then, but I didn't wear all black,
my nails and hair were always neatly groomed,
on weekends dressed in polos and perfume.
"You don't fit in," the Dean told me one day.
I had too many friends, too wide a pool,
and so I stripped the polish, and dove in,
deep into the dark box of the black.
Rehearsals filled with harsh Director's bark
until I broke, and rage I felt toward her
transformed me into characters so rich
in depth and higher than the limestone wall.
I rolled around in paint on a bare stage,
birthed Antigone in the stone basement,
pulled off Ophelia in a sandbox, too.
I was good, and known. In here, I was alive.
Not strong enough to last, and so, I quit.
A tragedy that ends in tears, like that.

Walked off the stage and out of the black box,
no theatre, a stage, or an applause,
no marked up scripts, was lost, a wandering ghost.
Theatre, mere shadow of a dream that clung
to walls, my soul. For years I couldn't see
a play, couldn't sit and watch a show, that's live
without the velvet tears that haunted me.
Today, I say, I want to dress in black,
in pearls, and heels, and sweet Chanel perfume,
to climb the stairs and sit under the lights,
to hold a bill and feel the actor's buzz.
Today, I say, I want to see a play!

Stones

words in air
hang
and fall
like leaves
turning brown
and withering
on chilled ground

while,

words on paper
stay
and bleed
smashed guts
oozing black
and staining
on the slab.

Both, full of power—
Both, very much alive.

Elections

Social Media says we have a choice to choose,
a voice to use,
whether this or that, or
left or right, or
life or death—

Today, I'm choosing:
leaf piles and snicker-doodles.

Water

Autumn days as thin as window screens
in open kitchen windows
dividing trees, dripping butterscotch leaves
and us, empty vessels pale and gaping
at the lushness, just beyond our reach.
Heavy hands steady on the sink,
warm water runs until it pools below,
quieting sounds of kids, but scantly
dumbing echoes of distant dogs.

Just across the river,
a mother lost her son.
He jumped from the roof to drown it all,
I didn't know her well, but I imagine as he fell,
not even the darkest black water could match her yell.
How many mothers, I think,
are clutching the edge of sinks,
desperate not to spill over themselves,
letting steamy streams run across dry hands,
feel nothing, but brown paper air in punctured lungs.
How many mothers are barely holding on?

The Eternal One

How can I, but a blade of grass,
floating petal without a home
compare to such a wild field of love,
the expanse of which bends
from sky to never-ending sky.

Yet, here am I:
tiny seed, weepy blade
frail from footsteps, careless hands
crying out for The One to come.

Pluck me, cup me, burn me up!

Toss me in the fire
that blazes field and flame
bigger and bigger—Eternal.
So I, like the wide open space, can bend
from sky to never-ending sky,
swept up in a blue-lit dance.

Ready

Twenty years of therapy—
Diagnosis Soup.
New doctor, new location
maybe this time it'll stick.
She shuffles through my history book—

wounds and secrets from the past.
Crumpled tissues in the trash,
green plants on the windowsill,
bowl of breath mints by the desk,
the book snaps shut, external

sigh, as she creaks toward me
in her chair. Behind the mask, eyes stare.
"For two decades you've avoided pain,
so, why are you here now?" I swallow
a lump—gulp, acid and tears
when out of my mouth I hear,

"I'm ready to heal."
And, for the first time,
I think, I actually am.

Movement

I had a dream a friend
looked me in the eye and spoke:
You are not stuck here.

And so,
I'm moving.
Small circles, forward bends,
sometimes painful as my body creaks to life, but—

every day
I wake at six,
climb out of bed,
light a candle,
drink warm lemon water,
turn on the music,

and dance.

Lambs

Little girl,
soft and small in a heap
on the bathroom floor, a lamb

longing to be held, and seen, and known
to nuzzle nose in a strong chest,
toss big emotions in the air,
to bleat out in the safety
net of hands, *it's not my fault,*
to tear down decades of self-blame,

and shake the heavy coat of sadness
that sends a chill from head to toe.
Is it the virus, or the years of shame
leaving all at once? To rest
in words: *you're safe here.*
pillow soft, to hold

compassion, for the first time
this vision of little-me,
another lamb to tend to—
with tender hands, and hot mint tea,
with lavender, with poems—
cradle quietly in the night.

Held

Though things in this life
fall apart without warning,
we are still held tight

by God, holy one—
strong tower, unwavering,
The Father of Light.